The celebration of Mass, attended by approximately 200,000 people, in St Peter's Square. The Catholic Church now numbers some eight hundred million strong across all the nations of the world.

INSIDE THE

BUILDINGS AND HISTORY

TREASURES

CEREMONIES

VISITORS

EVERYDAY LIFE

Published by Gallery Books
A Division of W. H. Smith Publishers Inc.
112 Madison Avenue
New York, New York 10016

Produced by Bison Books Ltd
Kimbolton House
117A Fulham Road
London SW3 6RL

Copyright © 1990 Bison Books Ltd

ISBN 0-8317-4925-3

Printed in Hong Kong

All photographs by the author except:
H.E. The Ambassador Fred J. Eckert: pages 17, 22, 34,
43, 66, 118
Bridgeman Art Library/courtesy of the Vatican
Museums: page 57
Chris Fairclough Colour Library: pages 67, 123
James Davis Travel Photography: pages 132-133
Photoresources/Photos: C. M. Dixon: pages 47, 58, 59
Robert Harding Picture Library/courtesy of the Vatican
Museums: pages 48/photo: Mario Carrieri, 49, 155
Scala/courtesy of the Vatican Museums: pages 52-53,
65, 70, 71
Spectrum Colour Library: gatefold and pages 18-19
Vatican Museums: pages 46, 50, 51, 54-55, 56, 60-61,
62-63, 68, 69, 72-73, 74-75, 76-77, 142, 143
Zefa Picture Library/photo: John Flowerdew: page 29.

VATICAN

TEXT AND PHOTOGRAPHS   JOSEPH COUGHLAN

DESIGN   RAN BARNES

FLO

GALLERY BOOKS
An imprint of W.H. Smith Publishers Inc.
112 Madison Avenue
New York, New York 10016

GATEFOLD: *St Peter's and the Vatican.
The elliptical arms of the colonnade
seem to reach out to embrace the
world. Clearly visible in the picture are
the Audience Hall, the large white roof
to the left of the basilica; the Apostolic
Palace and the Secretariat of State,
the square block and loggias to the
right of the colonnade; behind them,
the long galleries of part of the Vatican
Museums; behind the basilica itself,
the Vatican hill and gardens and
several other buildings and offices.*

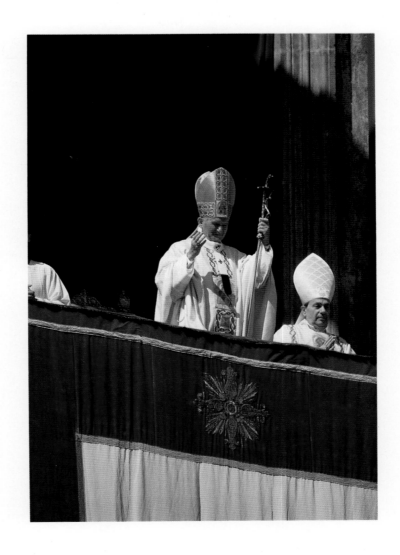

Pope John Paul II, the 267th successor to Peter the Apostle. Peter was martyred over 1900 years ago on a spot yards from where the Pope is giving this Easter blessing.

BUILDINGS AND HISTORY

Today we tend to think of the Vatican as the home of the Pope and as the administrative center of the Catholic Church, but these functions are relatively recent. The Apostolic Palace, the large building overlooking St Peter's Square from the north side, only became the permanent papal residence in the fifteenth century, after the ending of the Great Schism. The Roman Curia, the central administration of the Church, was only constituted into what is largely its present form in 1588. The reason why these 'hundred acres' are what they are goes back much further.

During the early Roman Empire, the *Ager Vaticanus* was a malaria-ridden marsh across the River Tiber from the heart of Imperial Rome. In 64 AD the Emperor Nero organized games here in his newly completed circus, which stood between the Gianiculan and Vatican hills. Peter the Apostle, the acknowledged leader of the Christians in Rome, was almost certainly crucified at these games. A substantial body of both literary and archaeological evidence points to his eventual tomb as being in the cemetery adjoining the circus.

In the reign of Constantine, the first emperor to allow the Christians full freedom of worship, a Christian basilica was built on the Vatican hill, probably between 320 and 333, on a site long venerated as St Peter's burial place. It is this tradition that has, over the centuries, never ceased to be the justification for what we see today in St Peter's and the rest of the Vatican. During extensive excavations, started in 1940, under St Peter's some remains were found that had been carefully enclosed in a funerary monument. This monument had become the base for the altar above it in the Constantinian basilica and subsequently for the building of St Peter's from 1506-1615. The remains were painstakingly examined and by 1963 believed to be those of a single individual, male, sturdily built, about 60-70 years old. Thus it is highly likely that the placing of the Vatican is determined by the existence of Peter's tomb; the Vatican rests, both literally and metaphorically, on the bones of St Peter.

The ascendancy of the papacy came about with the transfer of the seat of the Roman Empire to Constantinople and the fall of Rome during the fifth century. In 754 the basis for the temporal power of the popes was secured in a deal struck with Pepin III, King of the Franks. Several captured cities were made over to Pope Stephen II and the Papal States, as they became, survived until 1870, when the new nation of Italy was effectively formed. In 1929 the Lateran Treaty established the sovereignty of the Vatican City State within Italy and this is the form in which we see the Vatican today.

Throughout the early medieval period, the Constantinian basilica served as a center of pilgrimage and a monastery and also became the focus of a walled refuge, created by Pope Leo IV after the sack of Rome in 846. Remnants of these walls are still visible today, albeit somewhat restored over the centuries.

Repeated attacks on Rome by Huns, Goths, Visigoths, Saracens and Lombards left considerable destruction in their wake. The armies of Barbarossa succeeded in gaining entry to the basilica in 1167, massacring defenders of the church even on the High Altar. The Apostolic Palace was begun in the twelfth century, added to over a period of 400 years and finished by Bramante, who also worked on St Peter's. Again, in the thirteenth century, the fortifications were improved, hospitals built and the palaces and offices of the Curia begun. The first gardens were laid out by Nicholas III during 1277-80. It was also Nicholas who caused the famous *passetto* (an elevated fortified escape route!) to be built between the Apostolic Palace and the Castel Sant'Angelo, the mausoleum of the Emperor Hadrian which stands on the banks of the Tiber. Transformed into an impregnable fortress, the security this castle offered no doubt encouraged the return of the popes from Avignon to the Vatican in the 1370s. The former papal residence, the Lateran Palace, was now so damaged from successive invasions there was little other choice possible.

While successive pontiffs improved and extended the chapels, courtyards, gardens and palaces of the Vatican, none dared face the dilemma posed by the increasing deterioration of the Constantinian church. Nicholas V (1447-55) was probably the first to consider the complete rebuilding of the church, perhaps as part of the ambitious plans of architect Alberti to remodel the whole of Rome.

By this time the walls of St Peter's were up to six feet out of line, the roof was perilously unsafe and, in the context of the new humanism, the whole building was out of keeping with the vigorous, unabashed optimism of the age. It was not until 50 years later, however, with the accession of Julius II (1503-13), that Bramante was ordered to produce plans for the proposed reconstruction. The design was in the form of a Greek cross, centered on a hemispherical cupola, surrounded by four minor cupolas – not very different from the nucleus of the church that eventually resulted. By the time the first stone was laid in 1506, Julius had extensive other plans. The Sistine

Chapel, built during 1475-82 under Sixtus IV, by this time bore twelve frescoes on its walls including works by Pinturrichio, Botticelli and Signorelli. Much work was done in the papal apartments, following Piero della Francesca, by Perugino, Sodoma, Perruzzi and Lotto among others. Soon, under Julius, two major artists were called to the Vatican and created some of their greatest works here; in 1508 Julius commissioned Michelangelo to paint the Sistine Chapel ceiling, Raphael to work within the Apostolic Palace.

Successive architects sought to impose their mark on the 'new' basilica; Bramante died in 1514 and the original plans were adapted by Giuliano Sangallo, Fra Giocondo of Verona and Raphael. Raphael's frescoes dominate the Apostolic Palace and are more fully discussed in the section on treasures. His main contribution to the basilica, the lengthening of the nave, was later adapted. Raphael and Giocondo both died in 1520 and another set of plans was produced, this time by Antonio Sangallo and Peruzzi. Their contribution is difficult to assess, as little evidence remains either in the archives or in the building itself which is not attributable to others.

In 1527, some 80 years after the renewal of the basilica was started, the Leonine walls were breached by the armies of the Emperor Charles V. Once again Rome and the Vatican was plundered, its population subjected to massacres. The then Pope, Clement VII, took to his heels along the *passetto* to the Castel Sant'Angelo. His flight was effected by the self-sacrifice of his personal bodyguard, the Swiss Guard, the new shock troops created by Julius II only 20 years before.

Twelve years later, in 1539, the political climate in Rome now healthier, the foundations for the apse were finally laid. Everything of the Constantinian basilica except the transept had by now been demolished. In 1547, six years after his completion of the *Last Judgment* on the altar wall of the Sistine Chapel, Michelangelo reluctantly resigned himself to taking over the supervision of the works. He obtained from Pope Paul II a free hand in everything, albeit with little else, since his position was 'without pay and without reward'.

Seemingly Michelangelo determined to carry through the construction to a point where alteration would be impossible. Things moved on apace. Over the next sixteen years, his health gradually failing but directing the hundreds of laborers and craftsmen from his sick bed, which he had moved to the site, Michelangelo succeeded in taking the work through to the drum of the cupola. Having fought innumerable battles with new popes, with rivals and with financial and technical difficulties, he died on 18 February 1564 believing that he had brought into being the most important monument of sacred architecture for all time, glorifying God and averting 'a great shame for Christianity'.

But more changes were to come. In the year of the Spanish Armada, 1588, della Porta and Fontana were, dangerously as it would later prove, to heighten the curves of the cupola by fourteen feet. Under Maderno the nave was lengthened and the facade we see today constructed in 1612. The last visible construction of the fourth century basilica disappeared in 1614.

The doors of the central entrance of the original basilica were transferred to the new construction and are there today. On 1 November 1624, the anniversary of the consecration of the original basilica, the whole new church was consecrated by Urban VIII. The Renaissance spirit of Michelangelo's design was irretrievably altered by Bernini, on the instruction of Alexander VII, into a glorification of the primacy of the popes. His major works, the bronze baldacchino (1633) or canopy over the main altar; the cathedra, the gilded throne in the tribune enclosing what was once believed to be the chair of St Peter; and the colonnade (both 1666) really mark the effective completion of St Peter's.

New work, renovation and restoration have continued hand in hand until the present day. When today we see St Peter's, the Apostolic Palace, the Vatican Museums, it can seem at first that they are all of a single period. This is not so.

Visiting the Vatican, recognizing the Egyptian obelisk which Moses may have seen, that St Peter certainly saw, walking through Bernini's colonnade, past Michelangelo's *Pieta*, down into the Roman excavations, seeing the Pope in the twentieth-century audience hall, it becomes apparent that the Vatican can be understood in broader terms than any of these individual experiences. It is the site of the Curial offices of the Catholic Church; the home of the Pope; a series of perhaps extravagant monuments to a faith. All this is the fallible human side. Whether or not one is Catholic, however, the architecture of the Vatican can be seen above all as a celebration of human capacity, an extraordinary statement of optimism and of belief.

PREVIOUS PAGE *Across Rome the soaring dome of St Peter's, the spiritual center of the Vatican and the Catholic Church, breaks the skyline. Also visible are the towers of the Vatican City; to the right, the 'Radio Tower' and left, the Tower of the Winds. Both were part of the inner defensive ring envisaged by Nicholas V but never completed.*

ABOVE AND RIGHT *The gates of St Peter's are opened each morning to allow the faithful into early Mass. They are part of the portico designed by Carlo Maderno and finished in 1612. Clearly visible in the last picture is the silhouette of the obelisk at the center of St Peter's Square. This used to stand at the center of Nero's circus, the site of Peter's martyrdom. It was moved here by order of Sixtus V (1585-90).*

ABOVE *The portico of St. Peter's designed by Maderno. The facade, which is seemingly so much a coherent part of Bramante's and Michelangelo's basilica and the square and colonnade which proceed from it, was built some 50 years after Michelangelo's death and 50 years before the commissioning of Bernini's colonnade! Originally it was intended that there should be bell-towers at either end of the facade. Thankfully, however, the foundations proved insufficient and they were abandoned.*

16

ABOVE   *This is the corner of Bernini's colonnade, completed in 1666, at the point where the straight arm breaks into the curve. Directly beneath this is the Bronze Door, the entrance to the Apostolic Palace. Clearly visible on the 'shield' are the arms of the Chigi family, of whom Alexander VII (1655-67) was one.*

OVERLEAF   *This view of St Peter's from the River Tiber across the Ponte Sant'Angelo only became possible in 1933 with the construction of the Via della Conciliazione. Built to commemorate the ratification of the Lateran Treaty between Italy and the Vatican, this makes a triumphal avenue up to St Peter's. In the center of the picture can be seen the hospital of the Borgo, Santo Spirito. This was the area where the English pilgrims would traditionally congregate, the name* borgo *deriving from* burgh, *the old English term for district. On the hill behind stands the North American College.*

17

LEFT *St Peter's on Easter Sunday. Visible on the loggia in the facade are the hangings bearing the arms of the Pope. It is from here, after the service, that he will give his* Urbi et Orbi *blessing 'to the city and the world', since he is both Bishop of Rome and Pontiff to the whole Church. Just to the right of the basilica can be seen the apex of the Sistine Chapel roof; from here the signal is given announcing the election of a new Pope.*

ABOVE *The statues of St Peter and St Paul stand at the edge of the steps leading into the basilica, almost like sentries, but their size and downward glance to the level of mere mortals serve as reminders of the greatness of the Church.*

LEFT *One of the statues atop the colonnade. These are an integral part of Bernini's design, complementing the figures of Christ and the Apostles on the facade, and depict saints and martyrs.*

ABOVE *The building of St Peter's started in 1506. The last stone of the lantern of the dome was laid on 14 May 1590, inscribed with the name of Pope Sixtus V. The bronze bell and cross, together weighing 6443 lbs (about 3 tons), were hoisted into position in 1592. The arms of the cross are exactly 450 feet above the floor of the basilica. The* ambulatorio *or viewing gallery is a favorite spot for a panorama of Rome and the Vatican; it is reached by stairs between the two 'shells' of the dome.*

LEFT   The High Altar at the heart of St Peter's and the baldacchino (canopy) above it. In the foreground is the sunken area called the confessio. Directly beneath the altar, some 30 feet down, is what is believed to be the tomb of St Peter. The baldacchino was completed in 1633. The materials for its construction were taken primarily from the ribs of the cupola, which were re-covered in lead, and the bronze lattice of the portico of the Pantheon, a Roman temple built by Marcus Aurelius which had thus far survived largely intact. The glories of classical Rome were pillaged like quarries for the material with which to rebuild Rome and the Vatican of the popes. The commissioning of the baldacchino by Urban VIII, of the Barberini family, prompted a saying amongst anti-clerical Romans: 'What the barbarians didn't do, the Barberini have'.

ABOVE   The whole cupola, all 616,000 tons above the baldacchino and High Altar, is supported by the four massive piers. The actual height from the floor of the basilica to the arms of the cross surmounting the top of the cupola is 450 feet; from floor to base of the drum, the ambulatory, 240 feet. The inscription of 'Tu es Petrus . . . (thou art Peter and upon this rock I will build my church)' is in letters almost five feet high. The four medallions in the corbels of the piers are mosaics of the Evangelists, 28 feet in diameter.

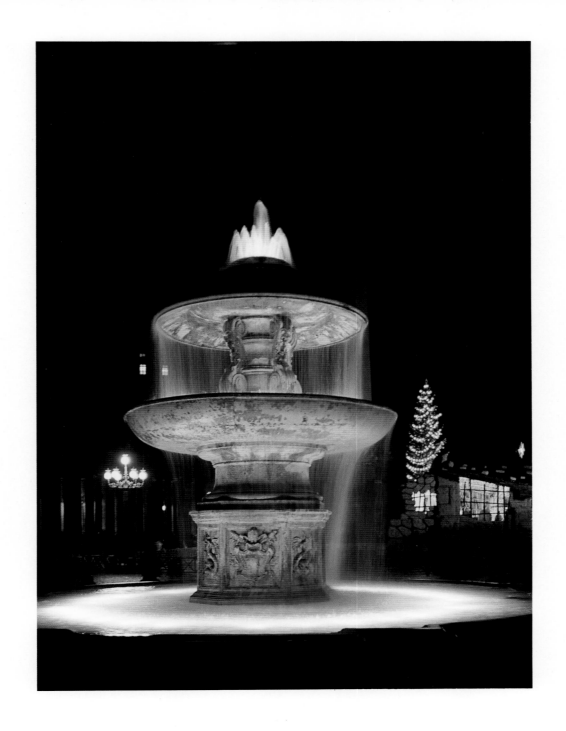

LEFT   *The Pope celebrating Mass at the High Altar. The sheer size of the basilica is indicated by the figures standing beneath the bronze baldacchino. Evident also is the contrast between the clean lines of Michelangelo's design for the fabric of the basilica and the baroque barley twist pillars of the canopy. Much has been written about the pomposity and the theatrical quality of St Peter's but this needs to be viewed in its historical context, as the product of a time when papacy and Church were being glorified in reaction to the Reformation.*

ABOVE   *One of the two beautiful fountains in St Peter's Square, not, curiously, built at the same time. The other fountain was built first, for Pope Paul V (1605-21), and predates the colonnade. Bernini's original plans called for a single, much larger, fountain between the obelisk and the entrance to the square. Liking Paul's fountain, he decided in 1667 to reproduce it on the other side. To the right and behind the fountain can be seen the St Peter's Christmas tree and crib.*

ABOVE   *The Palace of the Governorate of the Vatican City State. Situated behind the apse of St Peter's in the Vatican gardens, this palace, built between 1928-31, was planned to house a Roman seminary and to provide state apartments for visiting dignitaries. Now it is the headquarters of the civil administration, where the Council of the Vatican State holds its meetings. The coat of arms visible in the foreground is that of the present Pope, John Paul II.*

RIGHT   *The Vatican gardens. The villa or* casina, *little house, was built by Pirro Ligorio for Pope Pius IV (1559-65). This charming spot became the headquarters for the Pontifical Academy of Sciences in 1922. The Academy originated in a society called* Linceorum Academia, *founded in 1603. The members of the Academy, 70 in all, are appointed by the Pope with no regard for any ethnic or religious differences.*

LEFT   Part of the Fountain of the Eagle in the Vatican gardens, named from the eagle which perches at the top, an allusion to the arms of the Borghese family of Paul V (1605-21).

ABOVE   The centerpiece of the Fountain of the Galley. Dating, like the Fountain of the Eagle, from the pontificate of Paul V, the fountain was built by Carlo Maderno, the architect of the extended nave, portico and facade of St Peter's. The galley itself, made of lead, is a great favorite with younger visitors to the garden. It was actually added to the fountain by Clement IX (1668).

OVERLEAF   A general view of part of the Vatican gardens, seen from the top of the dome of St Peter's and showing the more formal, French area. Another part is in the more naturalistic English style. Clearly visible with the Governorate building and the Ethiopian College is the actual Vatican hill, which rises to a height of some 204 feet behind the basilica. In this westward view can also be seen, at the extreme lower left, the 'House of the Gardens' halfway up the slope. Now the headquarters of the Directorate of Archaeological Studies and Research set up by Pope John XXIII in 1960, it incorporates the remains of a medieval tower which may have been part of the inner defences built by Innocent III (1198-1216).

LEFT *The gardens abound with gifts made to the popes. This statue commemorates the appearance of our Lady of Guadalupe to Juan Diego of Mexico. The image was imprinted on the apron he wore when he shook roses from it.*

ABOVE *A bust placed in the walls of the old Vatican Radio building within the Vatican gardens. Based on the messenger god Hermes, it dates from the 1930s. Nowadays the main offices of the radio service are at the far end of the Via della Conciliazone near the Castel Sant'Angelo.*

ARCHIVUM
PARISIUM
TRANSFERTUR

ARCHIVIO
SEGRETO
VATICANO

ABOVE   *This bronze bas-relief on the main entrance to the Vatican Secret Archive from the Belvedere square depicts the temporary transfer of the archive from Rome to Paris (represented by the Colosseum and Notre Dame respectively) in 1810, by order of Napoleon.*

RIGHT   *A view of part of the Cortile San Damaso, the innermost courtyard of the Vatican. Enclosed on three sides by the loggias of Bramante and Raphael, this little square is the scene of many important Vatican functions, including the reception of visiting heads of state and the festival of the Swiss Guard. Overlooking the square are the corridors of the Secretariat of State, the Council for the Public Affairs of the Church (the diplomatic corps) and the private apartments of the papal household.*

ABOVE   *The general Seal of the Vatican Secret Archive. The new doors were installed in 1988 and fulfil a protective as well as simply decorative function.*

OVERLEAF   *St Peter's Square, without the crowds. The characteristic barriers that mark out the various sectors assigned during major ceremonies take considerable time to arrange.*

LEFT *The entrance to the Vatican Museums. This extraordinary double-flight staircase ramp (one for going up, the other down) was built in 1931-32 by Giuseppe Momo. It rises 18 yards over a length of 106 yards. The balustrades are decorated in bronze bas-relief with variations on the various papal coats of arms, for example at the top can be seen the five-balled emblem of the Medici family, derived from pills given out in their pharmacies!*

ABOVE *A bronze bas-relief on the doors to the Apostolic Vatican Library, showing the first librarians. The first librarian, Giovanni Andrea Bussi, was entrusted by Sixtus IV (1471-84) with the task of founding a public library, one of the first ever. All subjects, both sacred and profane, were considered fit for inclusion, in accordance with the prevailing humanism of the time. The works of the medieval Fathers of the Church and the ancient classics, both Latin and Greek, were included. Today the library is primarily a unique resource of manuscript material in both ecclesiastical and humanist disciplines. In 1988 some 2500 scholars and students from 46 countries accessed the 25,000 yards of shelving.*

ABOVE *The gardens are carefully tended, whether it be a Renaissance fountain or this year's crop of hyacinths.*

RIGHT *Sunset over the Vatican. In the foreground is the lantern of the cupola of St Andrea della Valle, the second largest dome in Rome – but there is only one St Peter's.*

TREASURES

The treasures of the Vatican. When one considers that the Vatican itself ranks in the 1960 UN register of world art as both a world art treasure and the greatest single concentration of art in the world, the normal scales of measurement, appreciation and perception are made almost redundant. Goethe, standing in St Peter's Square, apparently remarked that the Vatican had made him realize that art could abolish all standards of measurement.

Today many people around the world cite the wealth and riches of the Vatican in support of the accusation of worldliness so often directed at the Church. Well, that view is not new – St Peter's, Michelangelo said over 400 years ago, was a meadow on which many fat oxen had grazed. He was referring to the corruption and intrigue that the colossal building works had spawned. *Plus ça change* . . .

It is not the purpose of this book either to analyze the rumors and allegations concerning the Vatican Bank and its personnel or the collapse of the Banco Ambrosiano, or to provide a detailed discussion of the rights and wrongs of keeping valuable works of art in the Vatican. What is perhaps worth pointing out is that the Vatican runs at a loss, currently some US$40 million a year; all the income from the Vatican Museum goes to maintenance and restoration and to pay the salaries of the 250 staff who work there. The Vatican treasures and works of art are held by the Pope on trust. This was stipulated by the Italian state in the Lateran Treaty of 1929, which said that students and visitors must be able to view them, as the heritage of all mankind.

Canon law, the law of the Catholic Church, lays down strict rules for the administration of ecclesiastical property. The Pope may dispose, should he so wish, of any property that either he or his predecessor personally receives; any other property is seen as part of the patrimony of the papacy as such and hence of the world. It is certainly true that during the history of the Church the papacy has not always consistently followed the maxims of service, humility and unworldliness that characterize the person of Christ, around whose teachings the Church came into being. That, however, may be relevant to the history of the papacy and the Church, but does not detract from an appreciation of the cultural treasures housed, for whatever reason, within the Vatican.

What exactly could be said to constitute the treasures of the Vatican? There are a small number of first-rank works of art that spring immediately to mind: the Sistine Chapel (ceiling, altar wall and other frescoes); the *Stanze* of Raphael in the Apostolic Palace; Michelangelo's *Pieta* inside St Peter's; and St Peter's itself!

On further acquaintance the list lengthens to include the rest of the Vatican Museums, which contain distinct collections such as the Gallery of Maps; the Hall of the Immaculate Conception; the Vatican Picture Gallery (Giotto, Bellini, Titian, Veronese, Pinturicchio, Caravaggio, da Vinci and van Dyck); the collection of modern art (Matisse, Chagal, Dali, Gauguin, Klee, Kandinsky, Modigliani and Henry Moore); the historical collection of coaches, cars, uniforms, souvenirs of battle and an arsenal; the Pio-Clementine collection of classical pieces; the Chairamonti Museum; the Greek originals; the Etruscan, Egyptian and Pagan collections, the Ethnological Museum . . . and more.

Apart from works of art the Vatican is also responsible, in its capacity either as the Holy See (the seat of the papacy) or the Vatican City State, for the Vatican Observatory, Vatican Radio and the Vatican Film and Television Service, the Secret Archives (30 miles of shelves, all full), the Apostolic Library (700,000 printed volumes, 65,000 manuscript volumes, 100,000 maps and engravings and 100,000 autograph items), five Roman universities, eight Pontifical Academies devoted to arts, natural sciences, music and religious practices, an almost indeterminate number (100+) of seminaries, colleges and faculties, and 47 universities outside Rome.

The contribution made to the world's store of learning by all these varied and various institutions and collections is both significant and substantial. For example, the Jesuit astronomers of the papal observatories (either in the Vatican itself or at Castel Gandolfo, the papal summer residence) research, in particular, interstellar polarization and the classification of stellar spectra. It should be remembered that the Western calendar currently in use was established in 1576 during the papacy of Gregory XIII, from the Tower of the Winds in the Vatican gardens.

All of these combine to create the extraordinary diversity and depth of the cultural riches of the Vatican. Within this cornucopia, the favorites, the giants, occupy a special place; above all, Michelangelo's *Pieta*, the Sistine Chapel, and the *Stanze* of Raphael.

The *Pieta* came about as a commission from the French Cardinal Jean de Villiers de la Groslaye, in a contract dated 26 August 1498. The Cardinal intended that the sculpture should be installed in the Chapel of the Kings of France in St Peter's, as a souvenir for posterity worthy of himself and his country. At the time Michelangelo was young – only 23 – and little known, yet a wealthy Roman banker, Jacopo Galli, underwrote the work, should the Cardinal be displeased, with the words 'I . . . pledge my word to his most Reverend Lordship . . . that it shall be the finest work in marble which Rome today can show, and that no master of our days shall be able to produce a better . . .' A bold pledge indeed. Now, of course, we know that the artist not only fulfilled but so far exceeded it, that for millions of people around the world the word 'pieta' is synonymous with the *Pieta* of St Peter's.

When the sculpture was finally installed in St Peter's, very discreetly 'after dinner, as the city slept', it was without ceremony of any kind. The only immediate tribute was from the Guffatti family, stonecutter friends of Michelangelo, who actually transported the work from the workshop to its predestined niche; they refused payment for their backbreaking labor, saying 'we take our pay in heaven' – the best possible, and for a time the only, tribute the artist received. One day, overhearing a dispute over the authorship of his work, Michelangelo returned to the basilica and carved the band crossing the Virgin's breast with the words 'Michelangelo Buonarroti of Florence made this'.

This masterpiece of Michelangelo's youth was a realization of what he called 'the heart's image', the discarding of simple reality and its substitution with a set of puzzling contradictions. The Virgin is younger than her Son, a symbol of perpetual purity in the freshness of youth. The single obvious gesture of sorrow is her outstretched hand, and yet the whole sculpture evokes a mood of grief, sympathy and pity. While the Christ figure is life-sized, the Virgin, if she were to stand, would be over seven feet tall – and yet her head is the same size as Christ's. But these contradictory proportions in no way disturb the harmony of the whole. This, for Michelangelo, was the product of keeping 'one's compass in one's eyes and not in the hand, for the hands execute, but the eye judges'. Nevertheless, with the *Pieta* installed and duly signed, it was a somewhat despondent Michelangelo who in 1501 packed his bags and returned to Florence, there to create his *David*.

By 1506, Michelangelo was back in Rome and working on a magnificent marble tomb for the warrior Pope, Julius II, who then asked him to undertake the painting of the ceiling of the Sistine Chapel in the Apostolic Palace. The artist's only experience of fresco had been during his earliest days as an apprentice in Ghirlandaio's studio, and at first he resisted the papal commission. There was a suspicion of intrigue. The architect Donato Bramante, whose plans for the new St Peter's had just been approved, may have felt that the proposed tomb would threaten the credit and attention his basilica would command, a design that even Michelangelo recognized would not only be the most beautiful church in Christendom but also pave the way for a new and glorious Rome.

In 1508 Michelangelo reluctantly obeyed what was by now the Pope's command to return and paint the Sistine ceiling – the ceiling of what the artist considered the ugliest, most clumsy, ill-conceived and God-forsaken piece of architecture in all Italy. The chapel was a barn-like room measuring 132 feet by 44 feet, its pale blue, star-spattered ceiling 68 feet above the floor. It had been built in 1475-82 as a chapel-fortress with three-foot thick walls, high windows, battlements and soldier's quarters between the vaulted ceiling and roof. In January 1509 Michelangelo started work; dispensing quickly with any assistance he tackled its 5800 square feet alone. After four years the scaffolding was removed and the work finally revealed, largely at the insistence of an impatient Pope Julius II.

At about the same time Raphael, in 1508 only 25 years old, was commissioned to paint the Pope's personal apartments in the Apostolic Palace. Raphael was a less controversial figure than Michelangelo. He rarely, if ever, crossed swords with his patron and seemingly led a less tortuous life than his peer. The apartments, the *Stanze* of Raphael, as they came to be known, were on the second floor of the palace, in the wing added by Nicholas V (1447-55) to the original medieval structure. Many fifteenth century masters had worked there but most of their paintings were destroyed to make room for Raphael, whose work was continued by his assistants even after his early death in 1520. This in itself highlights one of the major differences between these two artistic giants; Michelangelo's work is largely by his own hand, whereas Raphael ran a studio, as was the custom of the time. At the height of his fame his *bottega* was innundated with commissions, from designs for a dagger to designs for the new St Peter's. His masterpiece, the *Stanze*, marks the height of Christian humanism. His handling of the medium of the fresco is quite different from that of Michelangelo. The *School of Athens* is fully in the sixteenth century tradition and the *Freeing of St Peter from Prison*, in the Heliodorus Room, is stunning in its use of light, much influenced by the Venetian school.

During the 1520s Europe was subjected to radical change. The universal Church was beginning to break into national units, and the papacy was humiliated when the armies of the Holy Roman Emperor sacked the city of the popes in 1527. It is hard now to envisage what this must have meant at the time, but some of its effects are visible in the choice of subject and the manner of portrayal of Michelangelo's *Last Judgment* on the altar wall of the Sistine Chapel. Fully six years of work, 1536-41, two more than the ceiling, were devoted to this. With Europe riven by the forces of reformation and counter-reformation, there is evidence here of the pessimism that finally overtook the Renaissance.

The masterpiece was unveiled 29 years after Julius II had consecrated the ceiling. Paul III fell to his knees before the painting and threatened excommunication to anyone who touched the 'glory of his reign'. Furor followed, and in time 'breeches' were painted over some of the nude figures. In 1541, however, as all Rome streamed through the Sistine, the viewers struck with the painting's impact, Michelangelo was the undisputed genius of the time. To many the Vatican is synonymous with his name.

PIVS · IX · PONT · MAX ·
LATERITIO · PAVIMENTO

LEFT   *The ceiling of the Gallery of Maps in the Vatican Museums is barrel-vaulted in shape. The decoration, and the series of historical and allegorical frescoes such as those seen here, continue the whole length of the corridor, all 400 feet of it. The maps themselves, 32 in number, were all drawn by the Dominican scholar Ignazio Danti in 1580-83. All the ceiling frescoes relate to the regions depicted on the walls beneath them. These were painted by a team of Mannerist artists under the direction of Girolemo Muziano and Cesare Nebbia during 1578-83.*

ABOVE   *This bas-relief of Medea with the daughters of Pelias is in the Gregorian Pagan Museum. The collection was only opened to the public in 1970 and was previously housed in the Lateran Palace. One of its main elements is Roman copies and restorations from the first to third centuries AD of Greek classical originals, 500-400 BC. The scene shown here depicts the sorceress Medea in the act of throwing a magic mixture into the cauldron that one of Pelias's daughters is preparing. The other daughter stands pensively, in her hand the sword with which she is to cut her father to pieces. The sorceress has deceived them into thinking that his body, if boiled in the cauldron, will be restored to youth; her real purpose is to restore Pelias's nephew, Jason (of the Golden Fleece), to the kingdom of which Pelias had robbed him.*

LEFT *This picture of the interior of the Mausoleum of the Caetenni below St Peter's shows exactly what second century AD Roman necropoli were like. The Caetenni, a wealthy patrician family, built their tomb near to the simple monument erected over the grave of St Peter – it is in fact literally yards away. It is still visible today and is open to the public for guided tours from the Ufficio Scavi, the Excavations Office. The actual tomb of Peter is now only visible through a tiny crack, well protected by armoured glass. It is nevertheless one of the most fascinating visits to make. To go from the present day down a series of steps and ramps through the very fabric of the basilica and suddenly find yourself on a second century pavement directly beneath the dome, the altar, and the remains of the Constantinian church somehow makes sense of the Vatican in a way no other excursion can.*

ABOVE *This detail from the early Christian sarcophagus of Junius Bassus in the Vatican collection shows St Peter being arrested by two soldiers. Junius Bassus was a fourth century AD Roman patrician and his tomb, one of a number which show scenes from both Old and New Testaments, is interesting for its framework of columns, creating a stage effect, and its classical sculptural style.*

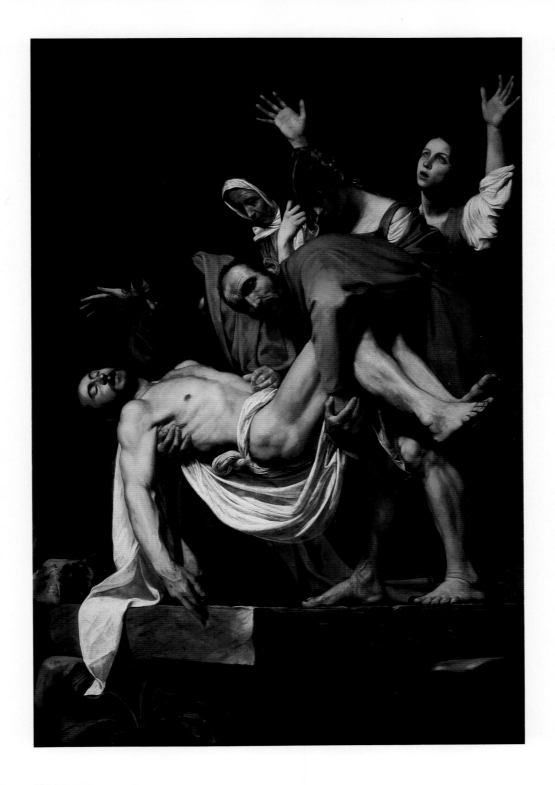

LEFT   *This picture of* St Lawrence and Pope Sixtus II *is in the Chapel of St Stephen and St Lawrence reached via the Vatican Museums. It is perhaps better known by the name of the artist who, at the command of Pope Nicholas V (1444-55), created it. He was Fra Giovanni da Fiesole, a Dominican monk, better known as Fra Angelico (1400-55). The picture shows Pope Sixtus II (257-9) conferring the order of diaconate upon St Lawrence, although the representation of Pope Sixtus is actually a portrait of Nicholas V. Particularly characteristic of Fra Angelico is the way he combines the achievements of the Renaissance with the mystical fervor of medieval painters.*

ABOVE   *The* Deposition of Christ *by Caravaggio was painted for the family chapel of Pietro Vittrice in S Maria in Vallicella, Rome, in 1603-4. It is one of the most important works in what is called his 'black manner'. Caravaggio (Michelangelo Merisi, 1573-1620) explored the problems of light to individualize subjects in his work. He heightened color and form compared to his 'classical' contemporaries and sought to achieve a complete and essential vision of nature; all brutality is removed from even the most crudely realistic images. The figure of Nicodemus (holding Christ's legs) is thought to be a self-portrait.*

PREVIOUS pp 52-3 *The* Dispute on the Blessed Sacrament *by Raphael on the west wall of the Segnatura Room in the private apartments or* Stanze *he designed for Julius II (1503-13) shows the Church Triumphant in heaven with the Trinity in communion and the Church Militant on earth venerating the Blessed Sacrament. The name of 'dispute' for this fresco was actually given in error, during the seventeenth century; it in fact depicts the glorification of the Church.*

PREVIOUS pp 54-5 *The* School of Athens, *also by Raphael, is an interesting contrast to the* Dispute. *Painted only a short time later, the style has lost any uncertainty and is perhaps one of the best examples of the spirit of Christian humanism prevailing at the time. The picture shows an imagined meeting of the most famous philosophers of classical times. Plato and Aristotle are seen presiding over the school under the arches and vaults of a vast basilica, the design of which prefigures Bramante's drawings for St Peter's.*

LEFT *This picture of one of the modern storerooms in the Vatican Secret Archive shows just a small part of the 30 miles of shelves occupied by archive material. The archive as it exists today was established by Pope Paul V in 1612. The term 'secret' in the official title dates from the days when secret archives were specifically those of a sovereign. They were regarded as private and only to be used for state or government purposes. Nowadays most of the archives are open for consultation by scholars and students. They contain all the acts and documents relating to the government of the Church.*

ABOVE *Dido, Queen of Carthage, prepares to make a sacrifice, from the early fifth century illustrated manuscript of Virgil's* Aeneid, *in the Vatican library. Dido loved and was abandoned by Aeneas, the founder of Rome, and killed herself in despair. The Vatican Virgil is one of only a very few illustrated classical books which survive as originals rather than later copies.*

OVERLEAF pp 60-1 *One of the two frescoes in the Pauline Chapel, the* Crucifixion of St Peter *by Michelangelo is particularly interesting in the way the saint, although nailed to the cross, is not writhing in pain but rather transfixes the viewer with an anguished and accusing gaze. The poses, the crush of bodies parallel to the picture plane, the flat light, the lack of depth, are all characteristic of the new Mannerist style. It was largely Michelangelo's work which was responsible for this school.*

OVERLEAF pp 62-3 *The* Conversion of St Paul, *together with the* Crucifixion of St Peter, *was Michelangelo's final work as a painter. Although relatively small, each some 20 by 21 feet, these two frescoes took eight years to complete, twice as long as the Sistine ceiling. This was probably due to his commitments as architect of St Peter's, ill-health and a backlog of other work. The style is still vigorous, the figures even more massive, the colors even brighter than in the Sistine Chapel. Many people believe that in the face of the stricken Paul there is a self-portrait of Michelangelo, racked with doubt.*

RIGHT *The* Laocoon, *one of the most powerful sculptures in the Vatican collection, is a legendary work of Greek art from around the beginning of the Christian era. It is known that Michelangelo admired it greatly, and it probably influenced his own sculpture. Attributed to the Rhodian sculptors Hagesandros, Polydoros and Athenodoros, it shows the fate of Laocoon and his two sons. According to Virgil in the Aeneid, Laocoon warned the Trojans against the Wooden Horse, arousing the hatred of the goddess Athena, who sent the serpents. The fate of both Laocoon and Troy was decreed and therefore inevitable. The original right arm was only found in 1905 and was added in 1957, replacing a reconstruction by Michelangelo which had served for the intervening 450 years!*

ABOVE *This detail from what is surely one of the best known classical paintings in existence is thought to represent Alexander the Great's wedding to Roxanne, and is probably a Roman copy of a famous painting by Aetion, a Greek artist of the time of Alexander. It was discovered on the Esquiline hill in 1605 and kept in the Villa Aldobrandini until 1818, when it passed to the Vatican Library.*

LEFT   *The relics of St Peter's. One day each year all the relics in their reliquaries are displayed at the High Altar. The veneration of relics continues much more strongly in the Latin nations of Europe than elsewhere. The classical custom of conserving cloths soaked in the blood of loved relatives or gladiators killed in the arena was continued with the* linteamina *or* brandea, *small pieces of cloth soaked in the blood of the martyrs. Some of these may be seen in the Sancta Sanctorum display next to the Sala dei Paramenti in the Vatican Museum. A later adaptation was to place an object in proximity to an acknowledged relic, as with the niche of the Pallia, opposite.*

ABOVE   *This little niche, the Niche of the Pallia, containing a gilded casket, has as its back wall a mosaic of Christ which dates from the ninth century. The niche is in the open space, the* confessio, *just in front of the High Altar and is actually directly over the tomb of St Peter. It was a common medieval act of veneration to lower a piece of cloth down a shaft to touch the Apostle's tomb and thus become a relic of it. The continuation of the practice by placing the pallia (long, strip-like vestments bestowed on newly instaled archbishops) here indicates the degree to which the place is revered.*

ABOVE *A rather different treatment of the theme of* Madonna and Child *from that of Michelangelo's* Pieta. *This nineteenth century glass painting is actually exhibited in the Museum, not as a window. The regally enthroned Virgin, whose expression indicates knowledge of her son's future, and the over-wise face of the son, show a stylized approach which is the opposite of Michelangelo.*

RIGHT *The* Pieta, *the masterpiece of Michelangelo's youth, rests in a little chapel, the first one on the right as you enter St Peter's. One of the most famous sculptures in the world, it was first installed in the Constantinian basilica without ceremony of any kind. Now the sculpture is recognized as marking a high point in the history of interpretation of human emotion. Interestingly it is the only surviving work that the artist signed, on the band crossing the Virgin's breast. He is believed to have overheard a conversation discussing the authorship of his work and his was not one of the names mentioned!*

LEFT and ABOVE   *The* Last Judgment *by Michelangelo, painted between 1536-41, sweeps over the altar wall of the Sistine Chapel. At its center a beardless Christ as Judge personifies the wrath of the Last Day, in contrast to the ceiling, where the predominant feeling is of a Creator Father supporting his children. The painting alludes to the Council to be convoked at Trent where the theological issues raised by the Reformation were to be* discussed. *By this time it seems that Michelangelo himself was becoming more deeply interested in the problems of theology than those of art; here composition and form are less important than content. Christ is surrounded by the Virgin Mary, and the martyrs. Below, to Christ's right and on a smaller scale, the blessed souls ascend to heaven, while to the left the damned descend, aided by clawed demons, to the waiting Charon,* guardian of Hades. *Oddly, the gates of hell gape open directly above the altar. There are several portraits in the picture, notably that of Monsignior Biagio Martinelli, the Pope's Master of Ceremonies. His features are given to Charon, with asses' ears, since the hapless priest had criticized aspects of Michelangelo's work. The painter himself is caricatured in the flayed skin of St Bartholemew, seated to the lower left of Christ.*

LEFT   The ceiling of the Sistine Chapel, Michelangelo's crowning glory as a painter, was produced between 1508 and 1512. The original instruction from Julius II was for the Twelve Apostles and additional (space-filling) decoration. The artist had completed a seventh of the total area when he adopted as his subject the beginnings of man and the world. The ceiling is broken down into three zones. The lunettes show the ancestors of Christ, pre-Redemption humanity. Between the lunettes are the Old Testament prophets, representing the human spirit inspired with the vision of the Redeemer to come. The central area of nine panels, four major, five minor, shows scenes from Genesis. The choice of scenes reflects the Renaissance ideal of life as a journey from body to spirit, from the creation of the universe to the new life on earth begun by Noah. The separation of light from darkness is placed over the altar, close to God, the drunkenness of Noah farthest away. It is noticeable that as Michelangelo's confidence grew the pictures became simpler, bolder and more expressive.

ABOVE   The central point, aesthetically and conceptually, of the whole Sistine ceiling is this detail from the Creation of Adam. The sense of power flowing from the Creator and the impotent yearning of Adam is evident here in just these two hands.

OVERLEAF   The following pages show the whole panel of the Creation of Adam, the Creation of Sun, Moon and Planets, and the Deluge or Flood. This last was almost certainly the first of the Genesis scenes to be painted; for the distance from which the panel is viewed, 68 feet, the figures are too small and too tightly drawn, and the colours too are subdued. This last factor is now the subject of considerable debate. At the time of writing the Sistine Chapel ceiling is undergoing a massive restoration. Opinions are hotly divided over the merits or otherwise of the result. Whether the restoration is accurate or desirable is difficult to assess; what is certain is that Michelangelo's work is as much in the forefront of public debate as it was almost 500 years

CEREMONIES

Central to the public image of the Vatican is the pomp and circumstance that seems to surround the papacy. The major festivals of the Catholic Church that take place in or outside St Peter's contain without doubt an element of theater. The Papal Master of Ceremonies, Monsignor Marini, affirms this but points out that 'the theatrical aspect is not, as in real theater, the suspension of disbelief; it is more like choreography, where the form is the means for conveying a more fundamental truth'.

There is ceremony in many of the functions, celebrations and anniversaries that occur during the Vatican year, often the product of centuries, indeed almost two millennia, of tradition. Today, however, much of the formality that used to surround the papacy has in fact been discarded. In a letter to Cardinal Villot, dated 14 September 1970, Pope Paul VI asked his then Secretary of State, 'in your capacity as our first collaborator, you cannot but be aware of our will to see that everyone who surrounds the Successor of Peter shows clearly the religious character of his mission, always most sincerely inspired to follow a line of genuine evangelical simplicity'.

Thus were abolished the Noble Guard, the Palatine Guard and the Pontifical Gendarmes, or civil guard, whose flamboyant uniforms and quasi-military purpose detracted, in the view of Paul VI, from the true character of the Holy See. The imperial style of the decorations in the Apostolic Palace, in burgundy and gold, gave way to a more sober color scheme of beige and grey. Under John Paul I the *sedia gestatoria*, or elevated throne, ceased to be used, as did the papal triple crown; John Paul I, the smiling pope, was installed as pastor, not prince.

Today the successors to the civil guard are clothed in a discreet but smart navy blue uniform of simple style – no more the wafting ostrich feathers preceding the papal presence, no more the embroidered canopy held aloft over the Pontiff's head. What ceremony remains is geared less to glorifying the Pope than to expressing the joy of believers in their faith and solemnizing the sacred rites and liturgy. For those who do not share that belief, witnessing the ceremonies is at least an impressive spectacle.

The papacy only comes to the attention of many people when the incumbent pope dies and the whole process of the election of his successor moves into gear. At one level, just as in the celebration of the Mass, this is ceremony. But what ceremony remains surrounding the death of a pope and the election and confirmation of his successor is not a public display surrounding particular individuals but is focused on the office of the papacy as such, the condition of the church and directions for the future.

When the Pope dies it is for the Cardinal Chamberlain to solemnly declare 'Yes, the Pope is dead'. Eighteen days later, after Masses have been offered for the deceased Pope, the College of Cardinals, the electors of the next Pope, move in procession from the Pauline Chapel (where they have celebrated the Mass of the Holy Spirit) to the Sistine Chapel. As they disappear into the area of the Vatican set aside for the conclave (from the Latin *cum clave*, meaning 'closed by key') people are already starting to gather in St Peter's Square below. At the exclamation *'Extra omnes!'*, 'Everyone out', all the doors, windows and any other means of access to the conclave area are bolted. The 120 cardinals now conduct the ballot and, until the necessary two-thirds-plus-one majority is reached, they will remain locked away from any external influence.

The famous sign of the *sfumata*, the curl of black or white smoke, is caused by the burning of the votes once the decision is made. In the past the votes were burned either with or without straw to cause the coloration; nowadays two chemicals known for their color-producing qualities are used. With the puff of white smoke the signal is given – by now, perhaps a day or even a week into the election, crowds gather whenever they can – and a roar sweeps across the square.

Robed in a white cassock, the new Pope will be proclaimed from the loggia of St Peter's, *'Habemus Papam'*, and he then makes his first appearance as Pope. The English Cardinal Basil Hume, Archbishop of Westminster, said at one of the elections of 1978 how aware he and his fellow cardinals were of the 'tremendous, terrifying responsibility' the election entailed.

The Pope is generally the central figure in all the Vatican ceremonies, the only exception being the swearing in of the new members of the Swiss Guard, which takes place in the Cortile San Damaso every 6 May. This is the anniversary of the massacre of their comrades in 1527. Their lives were given to protect Pope Clement VII, and give him enough time to escape along the *passetto* to the Castel Sant'Angelo. Even at this ceremony it is the celebration of the saving of the Pope that is central to the occasion.

There are, of course, many special Masses during the year. Palm Sunday, with the palms held aloft and candlelit ceremonies, is particularly visually striking. In addition to the festivals of Easter and Christmas, there are a number of Beatifications and Canonizations, when particular people, usually long dead and subject to years of research from the Causes of Saints' Commission, are acknowledged to have been particularly blessed or close to God. During the warmer months the celebrations take place in St Peter's Square.

In addition to the religious celebrations, there are ceremonies of a rather different sort. By virtue of its position as a sovereign state, the Holy See maintains formal diplomatic relations with over a hundred countries. Why, one may wonder, does a religious institution maintain a diplomatic corps? The original reasons lie many centuries back, when the papacy played a very positive role in the evolution of diplomacy during the Middle Ages and Renaissance. Nowadays the Council for the Public Affairs of the Church is the body responsible for diplomatic relations. Representing the Holy See are either nuncios, who take automatic precedence at the head of a diplomatic corps; pro-nuncios, whose precedence among ambassadors is in accordance with their date of appointment; or apostolic delegates. Delegations and nunciatures differ in that nunciatures have a recognized official diplomatic function in the host country, while delegations do not. The diplomatic activities of the Pope today are broader and more energetic than ever. They are based on the unique status of a sovereignty that is independent of any temporal power. The role of a diplomatic representative of the Holy See varies depending on where he is posted. Pope Paul VI, in 1969, stated the role of the diplomatic mission thus:

> The primary and specific purpose of . . . a papal representative is to render ever closer . . . the ties that bind the Apostolic See and the local churches. (He) . . . is to keep the Holy See regularly and objectively informed about the condition of the ecclesiastical community to which he has been sent, and about what may affect the life of the church and good of souls.

Whilst the representative is enjoined to establish good relations with the civil government, he is also to make himself known

> . . . to the religious and faithful of the territory where he carries out his mandate, to forward to Rome their proposals and requests (and) to make himself the interpreter, with those concerned, of the acts, documents, information and instructions emanating from the Holy See.

Thus it can be seen that the corps, with all the ceremony attached to the formal relations between nation states and the Holy See, relates more closely to the local church than to the civil government. A representative may also act as an intermediary between nations, however, as was the case in the dispute over the Beagle Straits between Chile and Argentina, when armed conflict was successfully if narrowly avoided.

It is important to remember that, although a nation's diplomat may be on Vatican territory, he is accredited to the Apostolic See. The Vatican City State only maintains a few technical missions to specific agencies of the United Nations, such as the International Postal Union.

Thus the ceremonial investitures, uniforms, receptions, are all oriented to the central resident at the Vatican, Peter's successor. It seems that ceremony in the life of the Vatican, whether it be a changing of the guard, the exchange of pleasantries that diplomatic protocol requires, the formalities of office workers, clerics and lay people alike, the central celebrations of Holy Mass, the papal audiences and elections, all celebrates the value of the individual but points, with a curious other-worldliness, to greater values.

How does a cardinal feel, sitting in conclave, faced with Michelangelo's *Last Judgment*? What does a priest feel as he celebrates Mass in a side-chapel of St Peter's? What does a civil guard feel, as the Pope walks by and two boys start playing with toy pistols? The weight of tradition could perhaps burden some, could seem to become a reason in itself; the liturgies, the colossal crowds, the masterpieces of art. . . . Ceremony formalizes and makes immediate the purpose of the Holy See. As the Master of Ceremonies pointed out, it is choreography, not cynical but generous, and to celebrate the good news of faith is no bad thing.

ABOVE *A rosy-cheeked guardsman maintains cordial but respectful watch at a ceremony in the square. The Swiss Guard are the most colorful remnant of the 'old' papacy but it is worth remembering that they are real not 'toy' soldiers. In addition to their training at the Vatican those that return to Switzerland, the majority, will be as much a part of their national army as any of their home-based compatriots.*

PREVIOUS PAGE *The Pope celebrates Mass on the steps of St Peter's. In addition to the attraction of greater numbers participating when a service is celebrated outside, it becomes clear that the Renaissance and Baroque architects and artists responsible for the design of St Peter's and its square fully realized the impact and magnificence of such occasions.*

RIGHT *A cameraman of RAI, the Italian state television network, finds his niche between two memorials to martyrs for the faith. All the major ceremonies are covered by Italian television for networking to many other countries of the world. The Vatican maintains its own televisual service but stops short of actual broadcasting. It makes available inserts for other networks as well as complete tapes of particular events for private buyers – at very reasonable prices.*

ABOVE and RIGHT *Pope John Paul II at a general audience in the Paul VI audience hall. These are weekly events; the Pope listens to presentations and gives a short piece of his own, in several languages. Audiences begin with the sign of the cross and end with the Apostolic Blessing. But what does the Pope actually do? Briefly, he maintains contact in a very real way with all the hierarchies in over 100 countries, each with its particular problems. The information that comes in for his personal scrutiny is torrential and unremitting. The Pope is looked to as the last word on any of the problems affecting the Church; whether it be the challenge of modern thought to traditional teaching; problems of poverty, injustice, overpopulation; diverse cultural trends which may threaten traditional Catholic belief and worship; and a host of other issues. At the same time he has to handle the bureaucracy characteristic of any administration – all the different congregations, tribunals, commissions and secretariats. In addition, he has to make his own contribution in writings, addresses, encyclicals and seminars. As a head of state, he meets world leaders and important visitors, and must be interested in the initiatives of the secular world. Lastly, there is the importance of his own example of a life of prayer to both clergy and laity. It is an impossible job.*

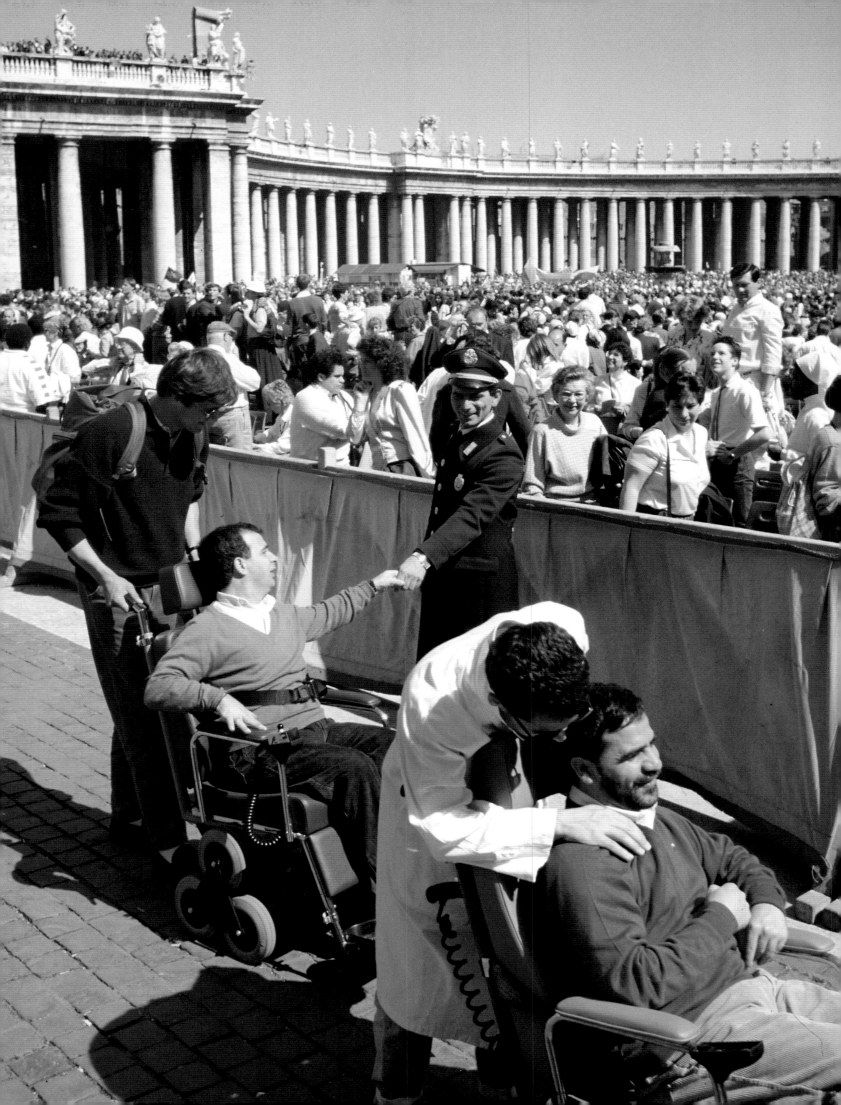

LEFT   *A member of the Vatican's Civil Guard, the gendarmes or policemen of the Vatican state, greets a disabled visitor to a papal ceremony. While the burden of vigilance is real and the professionalism of the Guard unquestioned, it is characteristic of the Vatican's security men that, once the object of their responsibility is gone, a genuine warmth is very much part of the job.*

ABOVE   *Major ceremonies at the Vatican are always enhanced by the singing of choristers such as these. The two Vatican choirs still extant, the Julian (St Peter's choir) and the Sistine (the papal choir) have their origins in 1513 and approximately 1480 respectively. Prior to that time the papal choir was the Schola Romanum, which was left behind when the popes went to Avignon! Nowadays the boys of the Julian choir attend a small school built above the sacristy adjoining the south wall of the basilica. They regularly tour abroad and continue to specialize in sacred music.*

ABOVE   *Priests from all the corners of the globe are involved in concelebrating a Mass on an occasion such as Palm Sunday. These priests and deacons will later move among the vast crowds giving communion. For them, too, this is a special day. To concelebrate a Mass with the Pope, the successor to St Peter, may be a unique occasion for each of these men.*

ABOVE *The Pope moves to greet in*
person the people attending Mass.
There will be some who, to get a
'good seat', have spent many hours
waiting for this moment.

LEFT *This nun, who has with her several disabled people in her care, observes a custom going back about two thousand years, the kissing of the ring. The Pope's ring, also called the seal of the fisherman, is the sign of his authority. In former days, when the ring's insignia was used to seal letters, it became the custom to break the seal on the death of a pope, to avoid misuse.*

ABOVE *Two nuns wait for the appearance of the Pope. Complete with binoculars, a useful item since the Mass can be so far away, they seem to be making quite a day of it.*

91

ABOVE   Despite the difficulties of attending a holy service amidst two hundred thousand people in a setting geared to the humanist spirit of the Renaissance, not everyone finds it impossible to pray. Many people, when attending a ceremony inside St Peter's or outside in the square, do find it impossible to reconcile a holy service with the scale of St Peter's. Nevertheless, these very problems are what makes the sense of universality and world community possible too.

RIGHT   Leading the service inside St Peter's, the Pope too concentrates for a few moments before delivering his sermon.

92

ABOVE *While her sister nuns are at communion, this contemplative nun finds a little private space in which to make her prayers.*

ABOVE   *During the incensing of the offerings at Mass it is clear that, although the order of service may be familiar, everything but the offerings themselves seem oversize.*

LEFT and ABOVE *Shortly before a service begins, the necessary items have been brought from the Sacristy. Logistics may seem a long way from faith but nevertheless play an important role in helping to avoid a shambles at a crucial moment.*

OVERLEAF *The Swiss Guard parade in St Peter's Square on Easter Sunday. A particular feature of this day in the Vatican's calendar of ceremonies is the presence of contingents from all the armed services of Italy. This commemorates the special relationship between the Vatican and Italy.*

97

LEFT *The officers commanding the Swiss Guard (in red) and the Republican Guard of the Carabinieri of Italy exchange the salute. This ceremonial recognition of the sovereignty of the Vatican dates back to the ratification of the Lateran Treaty in 1929. It is also representative of the Vatican's acknowledgment of the special efforts made by Italy to preserve the autonomy of the Vatican, particularly during the last World War. A feeling shared by many Italians, almost irrespective of belief, is that whatever nationality the Pope, he is in a special sense very much 'their' Pope.*

ABOVE *The great occasions and ceremonies, such as Easter, Christmas, canonizations and beatifications, anniversaries and jubilees, make possible not only state and diplomatic reunions but also personal ones. Contact between bishops and clergy, clerics and lay people, members of different religious orders and people of different nations and cultures is very much a part of the 'coming together' at a Vatican celebration.*

LEFT and ABOVE *Vast crowds gather in anticipation in the shadow of the statue of St Peter, with the press and television crews discreetly tucked behind it. The people responsible for organizing this occasion have a brief respite. Bishop Monduzzi, Prefect of the Papal Household, seems assured that all is ready.*

103

PREVIOUS PAGE   *Members of the*
Sacred College of Cardinals
concelebrating in the Mass sit out in
the brightness of a Roman summer's
day. 120 of the 125 cardinals – of
those 120, only those less than 80
years old – are the Electors of the
Pope. Of the Sacred College 32
cardinals are from Italy, 10 from USA,
seven from France, five from Brazil,
four each from Argentina, Canada,
Germany and Spain; three each from
Holland and Mexico; two each from
Australia, India, Philippines and
Poland; one each from Algeria, Austria,
Benin, Belgium, Bolivia,
Czechoslovakia, Chile, Colombia,
Dominican Republic, Ecuador, Egypt,
England, Guatemala, Hungary,
Indonesia, Ireland, Japan, Kenya,
Korea, Madagascar, Nigeria, Pakistan,
Peru, Portugal, Puerto Rico, Samoa,
Scotland, Senegal, Sri Lanka, South
Africa, Tanzania, Uganda, Ukraine,
Upper Volta, Venezuela, Vietnam and
Zaire.

ABOVE and RIGHT   *The Pope*
concelebrating with the cardinals and
quietly praying after communion. Given
the responsibilities of the papacy, such
quiet moments must be welcome.

ABOVE and RIGHT   *The central figure at Vatican ceremonies is almost invariably the Pope. The Vatican has never been more in the public eye than during the pontificate of the present Pope, John Paul II. The first non-Italian pope for over four hundred years, he symbolizes the changes in the Church in a changing world. His energy and constant travelling affirm his role as Peter's successor in today's far-flung Church.*

OVERLEAF *The investiture of new members of the Swiss Guard takes place each year on 6 May away from the public eye in the Cortile San Damaso, flanked by members of the papal household and the Secretariat of State. Grasping the standard with his left hand and raising his right hand, thumb and two fingers outstretched to represent the Trinity, the new member swears to serve the reigning Pope and his rightful successor in true and upright manner risking, if necessary, life and limb to defend them. A Guardsman must be a male Catholic citizen of Switzerland, single, over 5 feet 8½ inches tall, and between the ages of 19 and 25. If he then successfully completes his basic training at the recruiting school he can present himself for membership of the* Cohors Helvetica, *the papal bodyguard, one of the oldest regiments in the world with a continuous history.*

ABOVE At every ceremony there are comprehensive medical facilities available. This much-decorated old soldier has made his services available for almost 30 years.

112

ABOVE *These young people from Spain have just had their invitation to the Pope to come to Santiago in Galicia, north-west Spain, confirmed. There are many groups of young people around the world who respond very enthusiastically to Pope John Paul II. There is a new dynamism amongst Catholic youth.*

VISITORS

Through the portals of the Vatican City State people come and go to their work, to appointments, to audiences, to ceremonies, each one crossing each time from the Republic of Italy into the sovereign territory of the Vatican.

The Vatican City State, as presently constituted, came into existence on 11 February 1929 with the signing of the Lateran Treaty, the representatives for the two parties being Benito Mussolini and Cardinal Pietro Gospani. The purpose of the sovereignty of the Vatican City, both at its inception and today, is primarily to maintain its independence of any secular power. This was well expressed by Pope Pius XI in 1871 when, in conversation with the French Ambassador, he said, 'All that I want is a small corner of earth where I am master . . . so long as I do not have this little corner of earth, I shall not be able to exercise my spiritual functions in their fullness'. The role of the City State is not as heavily emphasized today as it was in 1929 but its existence is still sustained and protected.

The vast majority of visitors to the Vatican, other than those simply visiting St Peter's, come to see the Pope, which for most will take the form of a papal audience, either general or private. Others come to attend a papal Mass or to visit a specific office or person in the Curia, the administration of the Catholic Church.

The general audiences are usually held weekly on Wednesday mornings when the Pope is in Rome. These audiences, together with the Sunday Angelus led by the Pope from his study window in the Apostolic Palace overlooking St Peter's Square, and certain major ceremonies during the year such as Easter and Christmas, are the primary means for the Pope both to meet and address the broad spectrum of the Catholic Church. For the people who attend it may be the fulfilment of a lifetime's ambition, the culmination of a personal or group pilgrimage, or simply an occasion to see the Pope with their own eyes. The general audiences are invariably fascinating events. From eight or nine o'clock in the morning people start arriving in St Peter's Square where, weather permitting, the audience takes place. The other main location is in the Paul VI Audience Hall, a striking modern building designed by the Italian architect Pier Luigi Nervi and completed in 1971, a hundred yards from St Peter's.

From this time too the coaches start collecting in the square along the Via della Conciliazone. Traffic builds up, many a Roman temper is provoked, parking takes on nightmarish proportions as personal urgency displaces public spirituality. Traffic wardens coolly and sympathetically divert the offenders or, in the last resort, ticket or tow away the cars of the recalcitrant. Coach drivers from cooler European climates look on somewhat confused as their Latin colleagues try to persuade a warden or policeman away for a coffee to discuss the 'possibilities'.

Between these coaches one may glimpse a crocodile of school children animatedly winding their way to the audience entrance. Next to them a group of nuns, perhaps from South Korea, the Philippines or Africa, broad smiles giving evidence of their joyous anticipation at seeing the Pope, trotting half-enthusiastically, self-conscious of their perhaps unseemly haste. The myriad of languages from all corners of the world is heard in snatches or torrents. But no-one really minds. The Vatican civil guard, Swiss Guards and Italian state *carabinieri*, the wardens – they've seen it all before. In the process of checking entry tickets these officials have another vital task; security is stringent but difficult to enforce. Up to 12,000 people may attend an audience in the Paul VI Hall. For the major ceremonies held in St Peter's Square upwards of 250,000 can attend, possibly within striking distance of the Pope himself or other public figures. Since the attempt on the life of John Paul II, in May 1981, there have been extensive changes in security measures for the Pope's appearances. It is not hard to imagine the difficulties for the security staff, given the present Pope's genuine desire to be actually in contact, physical contact, with members of the faithful. Of course this is not only within the Vatican. The security forces of host nations, and particularly Italy, bear an awesome responsibility. It is evidence of their effectiveness that despite several 'scares' since 1981 they have thus far prevented tragedy.

So the people pour in. Bands play, choirs sing and then, with a moment's silence of recognition at the appearance of the Pope, there is a roar and hearty applause for the figure in white, who waves in response. He may perhaps be some hundred yards away, perhaps only feet, the response is universal. There then follows the sign of the cross; all audiences start this way, followed by prayers, a discourse on a particular subject and then an address to the people – all this in several languages. At Easter and Christmas the special message appropriate to that season may be repeated in 25 or more languages.

Towards the end of the audience the Pope, particularly the present Pope, John Paul II, comes down to meet those in the front rows and on the edges of the central aisle. In their enthusiasm to see the Pope close by, perhaps to shake hands, people climb on chairs, sometimes almost tumbling over each other. Otherwise demure nuns burrow through the throng to get to the front, babies are held aloft, newly married couples reach out hand-in-hand to greet the Holy Father. The eagerness is well-meant. No doubt some toes get trodden on but generally the mood is warm and friendly. Former strangers congratulate each other on having seen the Pope, groups sing, or chatter about their journey, their home country. Lacking a common language, gesticulation and facial expressions can be seen being used to get the message across.

Apart from visitors to the general audiences and major ceremonies, there is a constant stream of people coming and going for specific business at the Vatican. Since the Vatican is the prime organ for the administration of the Catholic Church, the majority of visitors are members of the clergy. The reasons for their visits vary considerably. A bishop could be on his five-yearly *ad limina* meeting with the Pope, to discuss subjects pertaining to his particular diocese, social problems, relations with Rome and a hundred other topics. Other clerical visitors may be pursuing a particular marriage annulment; the possible canonization of some outstanding person; a matter for discussion at the next UN General Assembly; the statement to be made concerning human rights in some sphere of social or political upheaval; changes in the manner of the celebration of the Mass – and so on. The range of topics is vast and the Vatican is involved in many different areas of activity all over the world. It is not uncommon to see a head of state or senior government official visiting one office whilst a representative of, say, the Romany people passes by, holding his entry permit from the office of the *Vigilanza* (security department) in his hand, looking for the appropriate door for his appointment to discuss the status of his people within the Church.

Another stream of visitors passes through the Porta Sant'Anna, St Anne's Gate, often regarded as the 'back door' to the Vatican. At this entrance the Swiss Guard wear their 'blues', not the dress uniform of yellow, red, and blue in which they normally patrol at their other posts. To a first-time visitor the sight of people passing to and fro at this point laden down with bulging shopping bags is something of a surprise. These are visitors to the *Annona*, the Vatican shopping centre! To be eligible to shop here for tax-free goods and groceries at prices lower than in Italy, one must possess a special card. The number of these cards is strictly controled, as are the amounts of produce that card-holders may purchase each week or month. The existence of this facility, and the low prices charged, is due to the presence in Rome of so many church institutions, colleges and seminaries which need this indirect financial assistance in order to survive. It obviously makes more sense to reduce state taxes than to divert real assets away from the support of the church around the world, the main purpose of church activities. It also helps lay (non-clerical) employees of the Vatican, who almost all live in Italy, to support their families on the salaries they receive, which are generally slightly lower than their jobs would command outside the Vatican.

So amidst shopping bags – and diplomatic bags – envoys, ambassadors, priests and nuns, crowds for the audiences, kings and queens, presidents and paupers, scholars, students and researchers come and go through the various doors of the Vatican. Some walk in wonderment, some weighed down with pressing concerns - all, however are a testament to the extraordinary diversity of activities of this pocket-handkerchief of land.

ABOVE   A gesture of faith. Almost all
visitors to St Peter's continue the
tradition of touching the extended right
foot of the statue of St Peter, the first
'Bishop of Rome'. The statue itself is
attributed to Arnolfo di Cambio and
dates from the thirteenth century.
Quite what are the origins of the
tradition is unrecorded. Perhaps it is
simply that the foot, being slightly
extended from the pedestal, 'invites'
people to touch it. The condition of the
foot shows that this tradition has
certainly encouraged a substantial
following!

RIGHT   Having studied for two years in
Rome, this young seminarian from
West Africa feels quite at home amidst
the Vatican celebrations. The number
of Third World students for the
priesthood is growing rapidly, unlike in
most of Europe and the United States.

LEFT and ABOVE *While there are, of course, a number of cardinals and bishops who actually work in the Curial offices of the Vatican, the majority are in posts in their own countries. All bishops come to meet the Pope personally every five years, usually in national groups. There are also less frequent occasions when the Pope calls a Synod or Council and all the bishops, archbishops and cardinals meet, nowadays almost always in the Vatican.*

ABOVE   *With their teacher in the van, these unmistakably Italian high school students seem unsure whether to run or walk to the entrance to a papal audience. Tickets to audiences specify areas or blocks within the hall. Within each block it is 'first come, first served' for the better seats, flanking the aisle, where there is a chance of perhaps talking to the Pope personally.*

ABOVE   *Waiting for the appearance of
the Pope can be a tiring experience,
especially on a Roman summer day.
This mother and her children have
found the fountain to be a welcome
diversion. In fact, judging by the boy's
use of a characteristic Roman
gesticulation, he's not quite sure
whether it's worth waiting any longer
or why they should leave the fountain
at all. After all they will be able to see
the Pope from there, albeit two
hundred yards away!*

ABOVE *A nun from the Philippines has secured her place next to the aisle set up in St Peter's Square for the Palm Sunday celebration. There is a growing Filippino community in Rome, as in many other western capitals. This particular sister has taken up work in Rome to help look after her* compadres, *many of them single women who work in hotels or domestic service. A predominantly Catholic people, they find the Church a prime focus for maintaining their cultural identity.*

RIGHT *The two nuns in white habits seen here work in the Vatican's own Health Service. While the confidentiality of patients is maintained here as elsewhere in the world, the third sister is no doubt anxious for news of someone dear to her. The Health Service, just yards away from the papal apartments and Vatican pharmacy, is manned 24 hours a day and has available the most up-to-date equipment. Vatican doctors come in from 'outside' but regularly hold clinics during the week.*

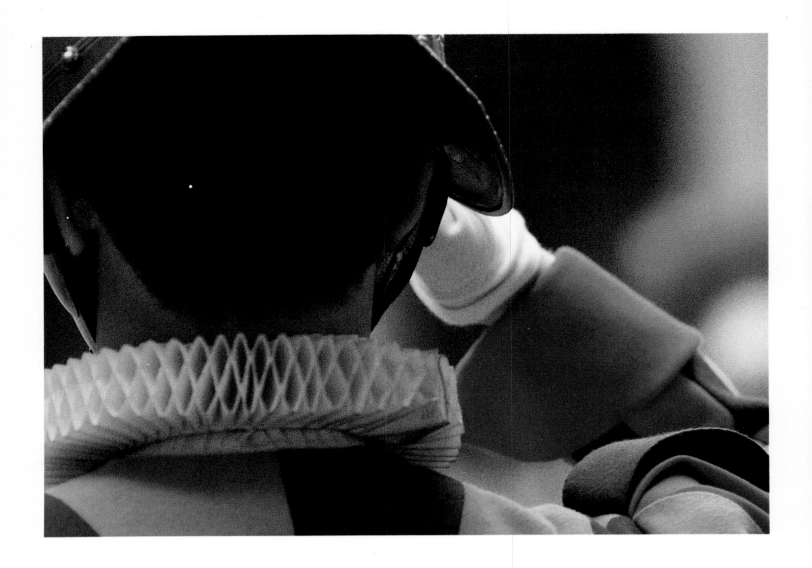

ABOVE *A guardsman of the* Cohors Helvetica, *the Swiss Guard, takes the salute at the commemoration ceremony of 6 May 1527. For many of those who serve in the Guard, there is an element of personal service or 'calling'. The guardsmen, all Catholics, swear fidelity to the person of the Pope. Some will continue in service for perhaps 25 years. The famous uniform probably dates from 1548, some 43 years after the Guard was founded.*

RIGHT *At the principal entrance to the Vatican, the Portone di Bronzo, Bronze Door, a halberdier stands guard. This door opens, well guarded, in the morning to admit those attending the Pope's private Mass. The entrance was built for Pope Paul V, in 1619, under the direction of Carlo Maderno, the architect of the facade of St Peter's. The actual doors, part of one of which can be seen here, were cast by Censovi and Beltranelli. They were hung by Bernini in 1667 at the point where St Peter's, the square and the Apostolic Palace meet.*

LEFT   *This charming young lady, from France, has just caught her first glimpse of the Pope. She seems more caught up in the spectacle of the day, an Easter Sunday Mass celebrated in the square, than nervous about shortly having to cross the steps up to the altar to receive communion from the Pope. At all the major festivals, a certain number of people will receive communion directly from the Pope.*

ABOVE   *Devotional prayer cards still figure largely as an aid to prayer for many of the faithful. This elderly gentleman had come to watch the erection of the Christmas tree. The Vatican's presence in Rome plays a major part in many Romans' lives; the year is punctuated by certain festivals and functions which are popularly supported by local people, not all of them believers.*

LEFT *In full stride, this gentleman leads the singing in his part of the square during a papal Mass. The many different nations that are represented at any papal Mass often point up cultural variations in the manner of celebrating Mass. It would be hard to imagine someone from northern Europe being quite so publicly enthusiastic during a Mass of a hundred thousand people.*

ABOVE *It is not always crowded in the square – at least not always with people!*

129

LEFT and ABOVE Members of the Curial offices come from both religious orders and the ranks of diocesan priests. Some religious orders have traditional ties to particular areas of Curial work. The Jesuits, for example, run Vatican Radio, and are found in the astronomical observatory and the Gregorian University. The Dominicans are found in the Congregation for the Doctrine of the Faith (once the home of the Inquisition) and the Angelicum University of St Thomas Aquinas. The Salesians are often associated with the Polyglot Press (the Vatican printing house) and the publishing house, the Libreria Editrice Vaticana.

OVERLEAF The view from the top of St Peter's. Like so many visitors to the Vatican, this nun has made the climb to enjoy the breathtaking panorama. At the far end of the Via della Conciliazione can be seen the Castel Sant'Angelo. Just discernible is the famous 'escape route' for past popes, running from the battlemented gateway just to the left of the curved colonnade to the castle. It can be hard to imagine how much this view has changed over the centuries; once a marsh with a hill behind it, now the heart of a thriving city.

EVERYDAY LIFE

The main gates of St Peter's open at seven o'clock each morning. Great iron gates part to allow access to the first public Mass of the day, celebrated in one of the side chapels of the enormous basilica. Only the lights high in the upper story of the Apostolic Palace show that the Pope and his household are up and about. In fact his hour of private prayer and the Mass he personally says afterward are already over. Another day in the life of the Vatican and the successor to St Peter is under way.

As the 'night-shift', primarily Swiss Guards, the Civil Guard and one or two other workers, make ready to stand down, there is a discernible quickening of tempo in the Vatican's 108 acres and its Roman surroundings. At this time the other principal gateways of the Vatican City also open up, the Bronze Door, entrance to the heart of the Vatican's administrative center via Bernini's Scala Regia, the Porta Sant'Anna, the 'back door', and the Arco della Campana, adjacent to the facade of the basilica, are reinforced with their day-time complement of Swiss Guards, their presence one of the most characteristic aspects of the Vatican.

The Swiss Guard, the *Cohors Helvetica*, founded during the papacy of the warrior Pope Julius II, have been in the service of the popes for almost five centuries. Originally envisaged as 'shock troops', with their fidelity proven during the tragic Sack of Rome in 1527, they appear today to be ceremonial rather than real soldiers. Although armed with pikes and halberds, however, these young men are highly trained and carry, discreetly, tear gas canisters, anti-personnel grenades and small but highly effective automatic firearms. They number approximately 120, are all Catholic and still come exclusively from Switzerland. All the guardsmen live in the Vatican, for a tour of service generally of two years, their quarters close to St Anne's Gate. Many, particularly the sergeants and senior officers who are also allowed to marry, stay on longer.

When in their splendid uniforms the Swiss Guard are perhaps, after the Pope himself, the most photographed members of the Vatican family. Off-duty they can go out and about, but are asked to be discreet. They maintain a soccer team which regularly does rather well in the college leagues. They also do rather well socially; the attractive young women of Rome consider a guardsman quite a catch.

With the changing of the guard and the opening of the gates the clerical and lay workers arrive, some 5500 in total, at their offices and studios, studies and workshops. The working day is 8.00-1.30, six days a week. Salaries and working conditions are independent of the Italian state regulations. What may be missing from the pay packet is compensated for by the possibility of subsidized housing, groceries and consumer goods and a petrol allowance. Goods such as alcohol and tobacco are carefully rationed and any abuse of the privileges swiftly dealt with. For most of the lay workers in the Vatican employ, there is a strong sense of service to the church, morale is high and there is frequently a long tradition of family involvement. Today, after the July 1969 reforms of Paul VI, conditions of work, salaries, methods of recruitment and pensions resemble practices established in more secular environments.

Of the 5500 people moving in and out of the Vatican each day, the lay workers number approximately 2500. Both they and the general administration of the City State come under the overall direction of the Pontifical Commission for the Vatican City State. The Commission, made up of seven cardinals, is presided over by the Cardinal-Secretary of State, who, at the time of writing, is Agostino Casaroli. On a daily basis, however, the minutiae of the work is handled by a cardinal pro-president and, in the capacity of principal executive, a 'special delegate', always a layman. Additional specialist advice is available to the Commission and its members from the Consulta, a consultative committee of eminent laymen.

The Commission is housed in the Governorate building immediately behind the apse of St Peter's and above the shop – a propitious location, it often seems; the Church, built on foundations of reality, looking toward a spiritual realization. To be fair, these rather grand offices were not originally intended for this purpose. They were instead meant for use as a minor seminary for the diocese of Rome and also as the state apartments for visiting royalty and heads of state.

While located in the government building and in theory subject to the rule of the Pope (who becomes on coronation not only Supreme Pontiff but also titular head of state of the Vatican), the administration of the Vatican City State actually devolves upon a number of ordinary citizens. The range of operations is considerable. The General Secretariat is responsible for legal affairs, general accounting, personnel, trading of goods in the *Annona* (the shop) and the posts, telegraphs and numismatic office. All Vatican coinage is accepted as legal tender in Italy; it is no longer minted in the City State but rather at the Italian state mint. Agreements determine the amount of Vatican currency issued at any one time. The stamps of the Poste Vaticane are not, however, usable in Italy, or vice versa.

Next in order of importance comes the department covering museums, galleries and monuments. This includes the specialist workshops concerned with mosaics, tapestries and the restoration of paintings and sculpture. General services are handled by a separate department and include maintenance of the fabric of the Vatican, the telephone exchange and cars (quite a fleet, given the numerous 'pope-mobiles' donated by various nations after hosting one of the present Pope's energetic visits). The Vatican, or in this case more properly the Holy See, also has its own radio station, televisual production unit, film library and, of course, press office.

It is worth remembering at this point that the Vatican City State and all its consequent offices, services and responsibilities exists to ensure the independence of the Holy See from any secular power. It is often difficult to understand why the Pope should need all this back-up; it can seem very worldly and at odds with the professed *raison d'être* of the Vatican, which is the 'Good News' of Christ. The Roman Curia and the Vatican City can perhaps be best understood by considering an 'other-worldliness' as fundamental. Archbishop Deskur, formerly head of the Pontifical Commission for Social Communications, put it this way,

> Religion has lost its place in public interest and opinion compared with political and economic issues. It has access to the front pages of the newspapers only when political or economic matters are involved. The mission of the Holy See which we have to communicate is to recall that there is a life after death. The church must work for social improvement but we need to transmit our *motivation*.

Thus the various organs of the Holy See in the Vatican City are to enable the Pope to communicate with the world. For example, the aim of Vatican Radio is to provide a link between the person of the Pope and Catholics throughout the world, particularly those parts where the Church is suppressed or actively persecuted. This can be difficult to relate to and reconcile with the availability of tax-free goods in the *Annona*, the enormous intrinsic wealth of the works of art, or the ritual of a Mass celebrated on the steps of St Peter's. It can all seem an awfully long way from a group of fishermen gathered round the son of a local carpenter – but then the responsibilities of caring for and directing the needs of a Church numbering over 800 million people *are* different from those of the early Church and the Vatican needs to be in part, if not in purpose, worldly.

So every day the offices open and close, telephones connecting the Vatican to far-flung corners ring, the heritage of its art is carefully maintained, protected and preserved, guards in Renaissance uniforms with twentieth century expertise keep a wary eye open, and all the time people come and go, to and from what is really, in the words of Paul VI, more a 'tiny pedestal' than a summit.

LEFT *Beyond the Bronze Door, the entrance to the Apostolic Palace, a sergeant of the Swiss Guard supervises the security measures necessary for the protection of the Pope. Stretching into the distance the Scala Regia, a masterpiece of* trompe l'oeil *architecture by Bernini, ascends to the Sala Regia, in effect the anteroom of the papal apartments.*

ABOVE *In the shadow of the cupola, a member of the gardening staff tends to part of the 30 acres of the Vatican gardens. The shrubbery, lawns, ornamental flowerbeds, formal paths, fountains and woodland require a substantial effort to maintain.*

LEFT *Cardinal Eduardo Pironio from Argentina, Prefect of the Pontifical Council for the Laity, starts another day's correspondence. The Council for the Laity was formed after the Second Vatican Council, to further the involvement of lay people in the affairs of the Church. The Council is part of the Roman Curia, the central administration of the Catholic Church, which consists of approximately 500 priests and religious and 50 lay people, plus the appropriate staff.*

ABOVE *Central to the working of most offices of the Curia is a weekly Congress meeting of all the staff. Here Cardinal Pironio is being briefed by the Under-Secretary of the Council on the preparations in hand for the World Day of Youth to be held in Santiago de Compostela later in the year.*

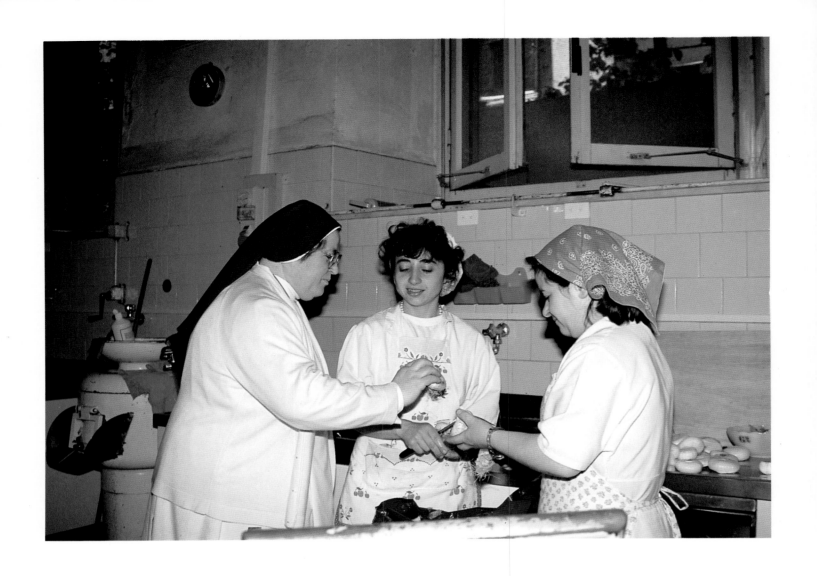

ABOVE   *Not all the institutions that come under the jurisdiction of the Pope are actually inside the Vatican, nor do all the personnel function simply in offices or behind desks! Here, in the heart of the Venerable English College, Sister Angelia and Signoras Pasquina and Serafina are preparing lunch for 70 hungry young seminarians. The duties of washing and drying are shared out amongst the students. Much of the produce used in these kitchens is bought from the Vatican.*

140

ABOVE 'Oggi festa! *Today's a holiday!'*
says Sister Mary Assumpta of the
community of the Sisters of Mercy.
Signora Fernanda Piacentini and her
cousin take great pride in their culinary
abilities. Every year thousands of
pilgrim visitors need to be catered for
while visiting Rome and the Vatican.
Palazzola, close to the papal summer
residence at Castel Gandolfo, is a part
of the English College but opens to
groups all the year, continuing a six-
hundred-year-old tradition of caring for
pilgrims.

ABOVE and RIGHT   *The Studio Arazzi,
the tapestry workshop, is never short
of work. The collection of Gobelin and
other tapestries is particularly prone to
the effects of ageing and is regularly
overhauled and restored.*

LEFT, ABOVE and OVERLEAF   *While the seasons of the year dictate the work to be done in the gardens, there is also a continuous effort to maintain the overall appearance of the whole of the Vatican City. The materials used are often specially prepared, as can be seen here in the re-plastering work being done on the wall of the Papal Apartments. It is not easy to buy sixteenth century plaster off-the-shelf! The members of the Sanpietrini, the body responsible for the maintenance work of the Vatican, are a tightly knit group. Often there is a tradition of several generations working for the Holy See, specialist skills being handed down from father to son.*

ABOVE   *As soon as the congregation leave a papal Mass the barriers and chairs start to be re-arranged for the next function. On this particular occasion the Palm Sunday Mass has finished at approximately midday. In four hours time the square and steps to the basilica will be completely reorganized to receive a vast number of students visiting the Pope. Note also the sign showing that certain forms of dress are not encouraged within St Peter's.*

ABOVE *In addition to maintaining an internal telephone network which is staffed by a very competent group of nuns 24 hours a day, the Vatican also makes available a small number of public call-boxes in St Peter's Square. Who knows what this young man has to chat about.*

149

ABOVE *Cardinal William Baum,*
Prefect of the Sacred Congregation for
Catholic Education, formerly
Archbishop of Washington, talks with
Kevin Grant (centre) and Dr Michael
Straiton (left), two leading Catholic
laymen from England. There is a
constant stream of visitors to the Curial
offices, sometimes offering help,
sometimes getting advice. In addition
most heads of Curial offices would
normally meet personally with the
Pope once a month to discuss
particular trends, world events or, if
about to visit a country, details
pertinent to the meetings to be held
there.

ABOVE *A last check . . . Bishop Monduzzi, the Prefect of the Pontifical Household, discusses any last-minute changes to the arrangements for a papal Mass with a member of the Gentlemen of the Holy See. The* Gentiluomini *are a group of men who offer their services at papal receptions, audiences and Masses.*

151

ABOVE *Within the walls of the Vatican
a fire could cause potentially
catastrophic damage. The* pompieri,
*firemen, of the Fire Service, are trained
especially in damage containment –
not from fire alone but also from the
fire control measures. All the
equipment and manpower necessary
is maintained in the proper state of
readiness; in fact the Vatican firemen
are often asked to lecture 'outside the
walls.' Note the 'SCV' number plate on
this fireman's little runabout; all the
Vatican cars bear this type of
registration.*

152

ABOVE   *Outside the walls, the environs of the Vatican have for centuries provided a steady market in souvenirs and religious bric-a-brac. Many visitors to the Vatican are surprised to find similar stalls inside the museums and even on the roof of the basilica. In general, thankfully, the standard of goods inside is better. Some of the offerings outside are very tongue-in-cheek indeed!*

153

LEFT and ABOVE *Scaffolding goes up
for the annual Christmas crib and
gradually comes down in the Sistine
Chapel as the massive undertaking of
restoration proceeds. The Vatican is
never completely free from scaffolding.
The needs of conservation, restoration
and special projects are constant and
the Sanpietrini are adept at putting up
constructions that one day may need
to be weather- (and vandal-) proof or
that echo Michelangelo's own
sixteenth century scaffolding
techniques.*

155

ABOVE   *Wednesday morning, two
hours before a papal
audience . . . and the Via della
Conciliazione is inundated with traffic,
particularly the coaches which bring
groups from all over the world. Scenes
like this attest to the extraordinary
popularity of Pope John Paul II and the
outreach of the Vatican and the
papacy into the lives of thousands.*

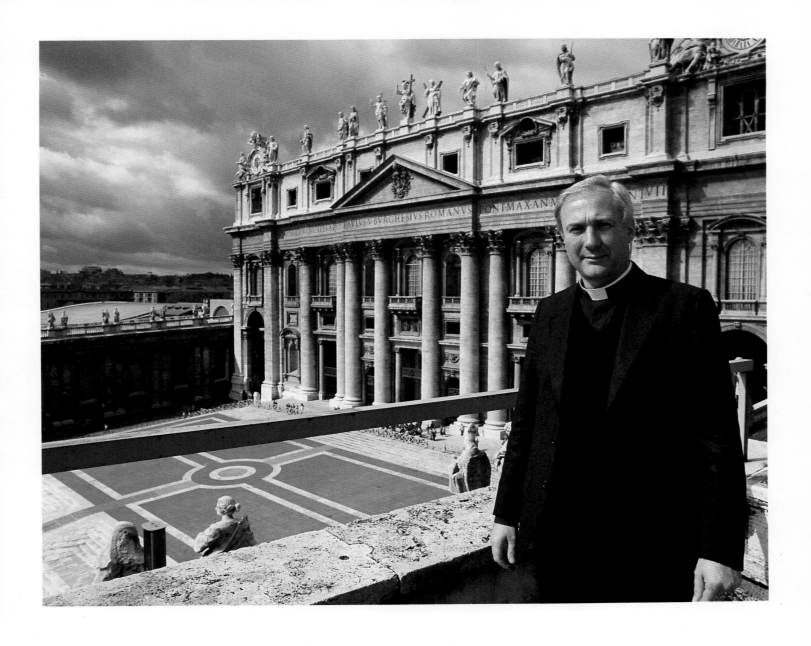

ABOVE   'The view from my office
window . . .' The peace and harmony
of this scene belies the fact that
Monsignor Marini, the Papal Master of
Ceremonies, is responsible for all the
liturgical aspects involved in any papal
function. From the placing of the
candlesticks and the lighting of the
basilica to the actual words used in
over a hundred different occasions in
any one year, all this crosses his desk.
His office window has probably the
best view of St Peter's, after the
Pope's!

OVERLEAF   Away from the bustle Sister
Livia, of the Elisabetine Sisters, calmly
'makes and mends', overlooking the
garden of the English College. While
there are a few women (lay or religious)
filling Curial offices in the Vatican the
majority, usually members of religious
orders, are involved in the ancilliary
services and in making everyday life at
the Vatican possible.

APR   2009